MW00568158

PICTURE
FLASHCARDS
FOR
WELCOME PLUS 4

Elizabeth Gray- Virginia Evans

Express Publishing

Published by Express Publishing

Liberty House, New Greenham Park, Newbury, Berkshire RG19 6HW
Tel: (0044) 1635 817 363 – Fax: (0044) 1635 817 463
e-mail: inquiries@expresspublishing.co.uk
INTERNET http: //www.expresspublishing.co.uk

© Elizabeth Gray - Virginia Evans, 2000

Colour Illustrations: © Express Publishing, 2000

All rights reserved. No part of this publication may be reproduced,
stored in a retrieval system, or transmitted in any form, or by
any means, electronic, photocopying or otherwise, without the
prior written permission of the publishers.

Illustrated by Terry Wilson

First published 2000

ISBN   1 - 84216 - 588 - 7

TO PREPARE YOUR FLASHCARDS FOR CLASSROOM USE :

- remove pages from book.

- cut along the dotted lines.

- stick the pictures onto separate pieces of cardboard.

- the corresponding words and sentences for each picture are printed at the back of this book. Simply cut them out and stick them onto the back of the flashcards.

- group cards into individual units (each card is printed with a unit number and flashcard number).

- store in separate envelopes or folders.

UNIT 1
lesson 1

3

UNIT 1
lesson 1

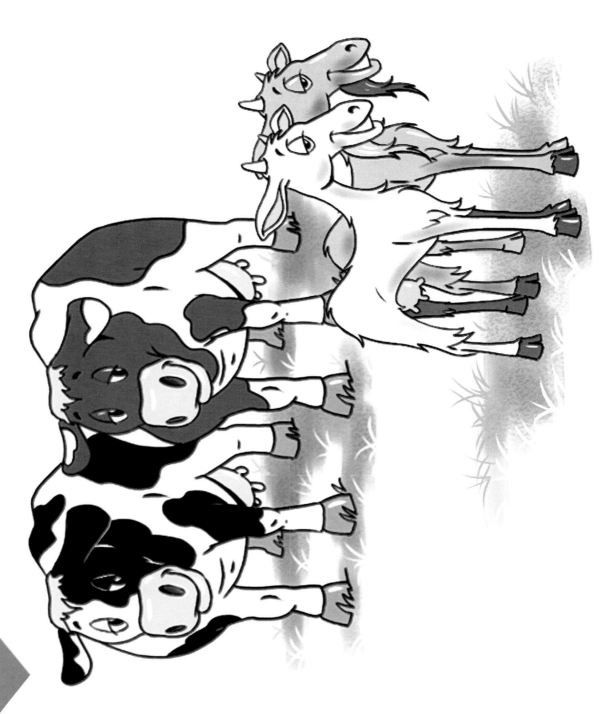

UNIT 1
lesson 1

UNIT 1
lesson 1

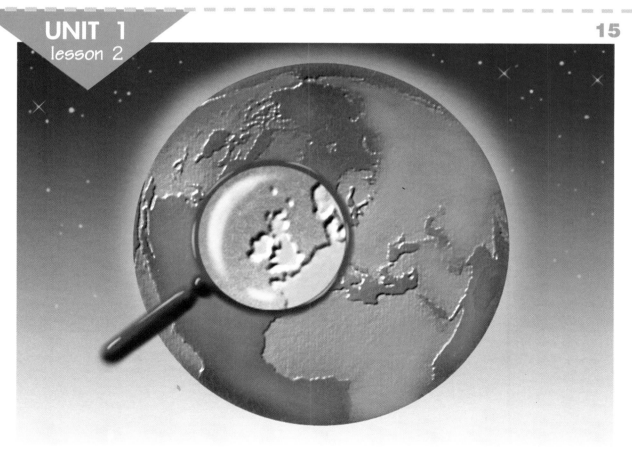

UNIT 2
lesson 1

UNIT 2
lesson 1

UNIT 2
lesson 1

UNIT 2
lesson 1

21

UNIT 2
lesson 1

UNIT 2
lesson 1

22

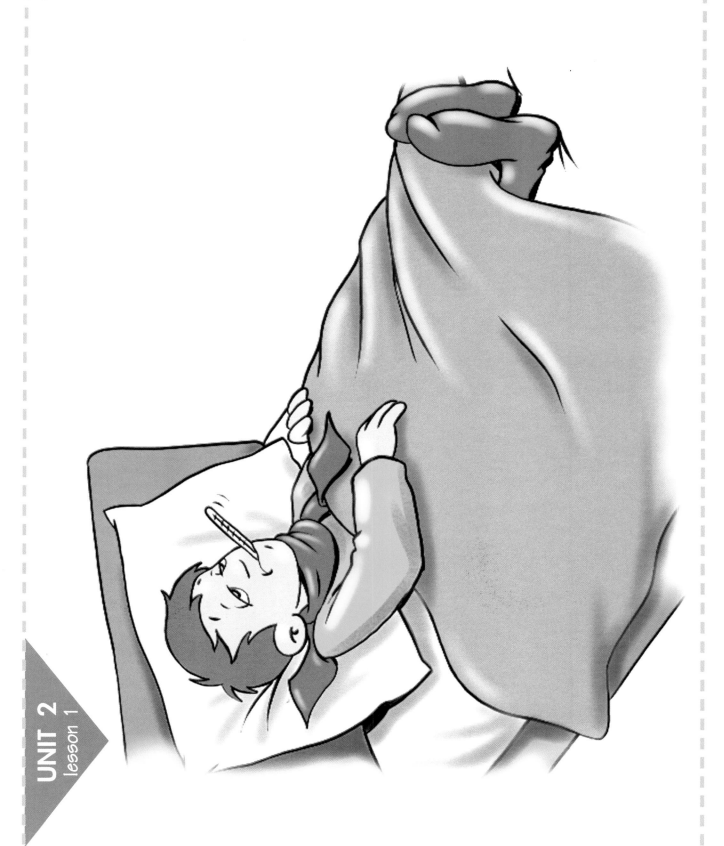

UNIT 2
lesson 1

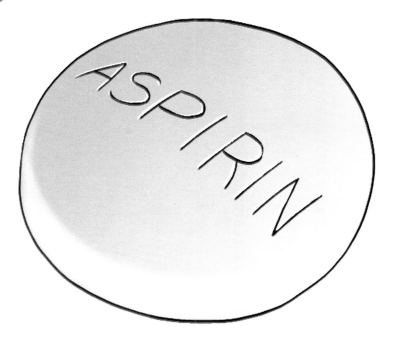

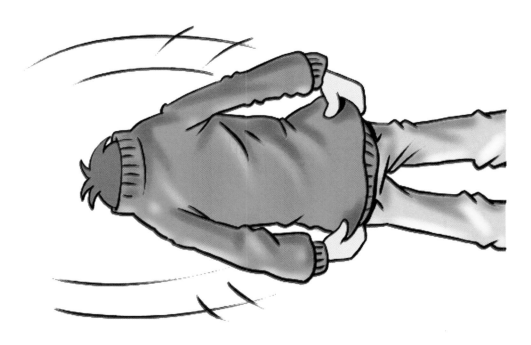

29

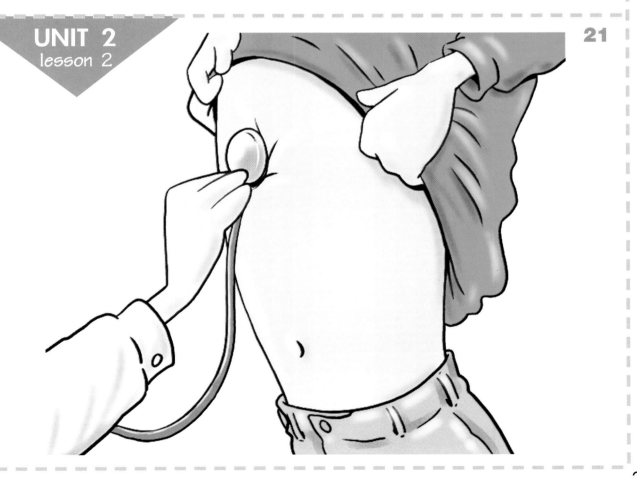

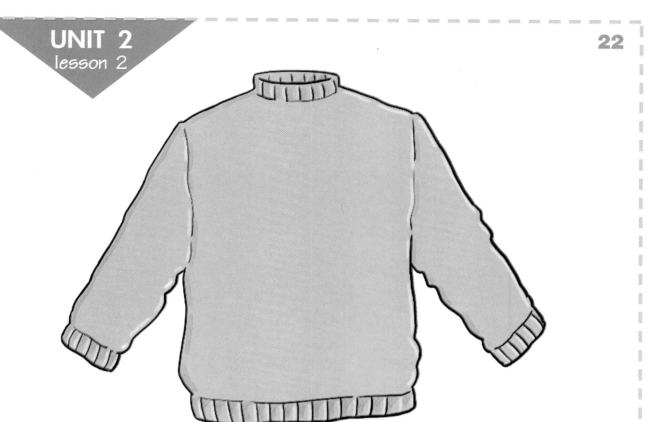

A-15B

ONE WAY
28D-45/32
TICKET

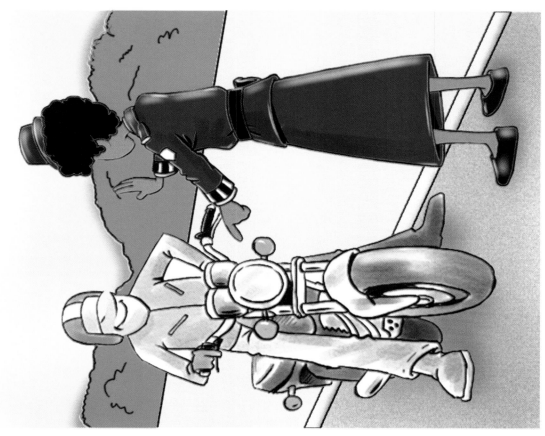

36

Wendy

Cindy

Oscar

Wendy

Eddy

Lin

Tom

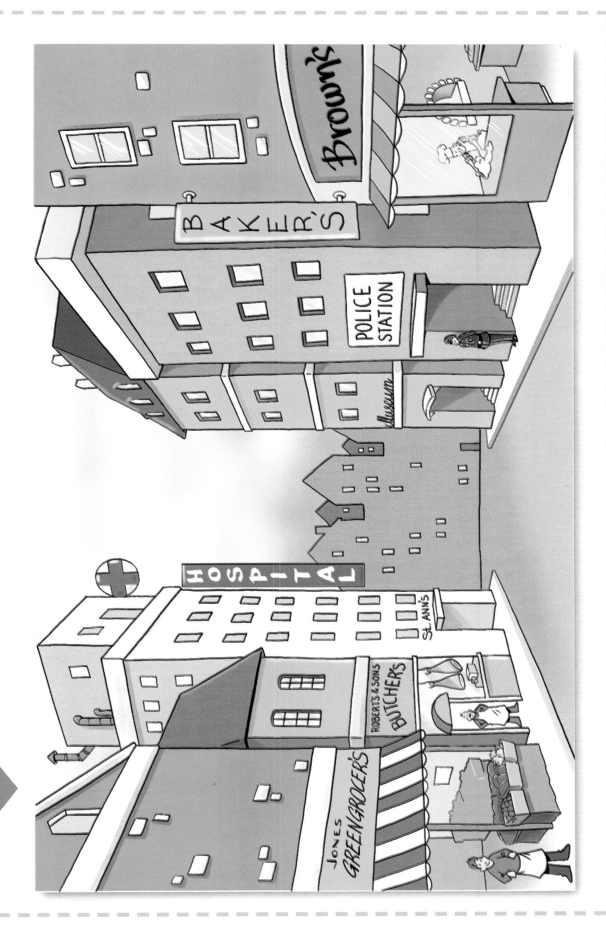

UNIT 3
lesson 2

26

UNIT 3
lesson 2

27

UNIT 4
lesson 1

UNIT 4
lesson 1

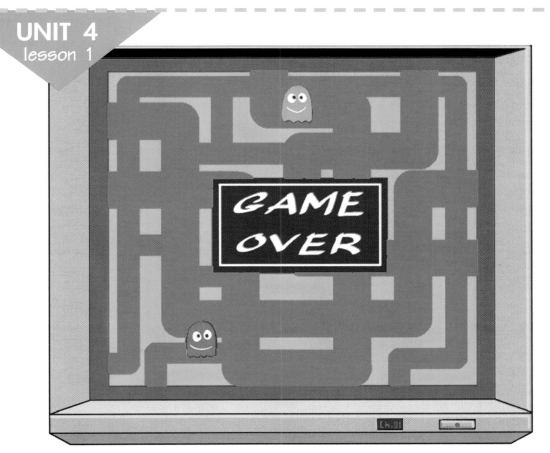

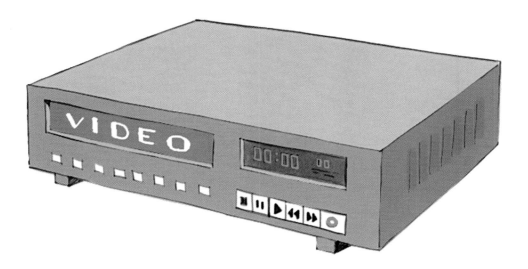

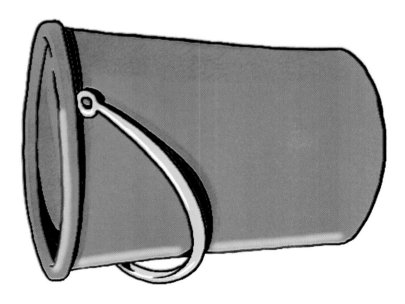

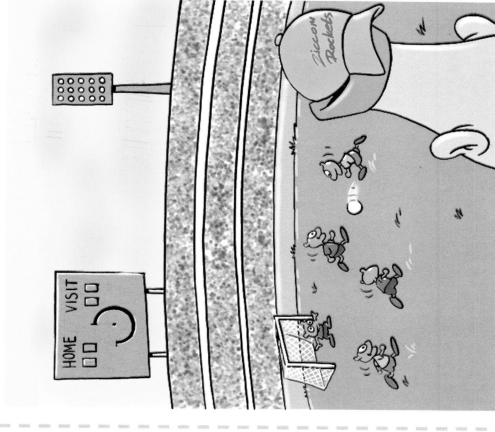

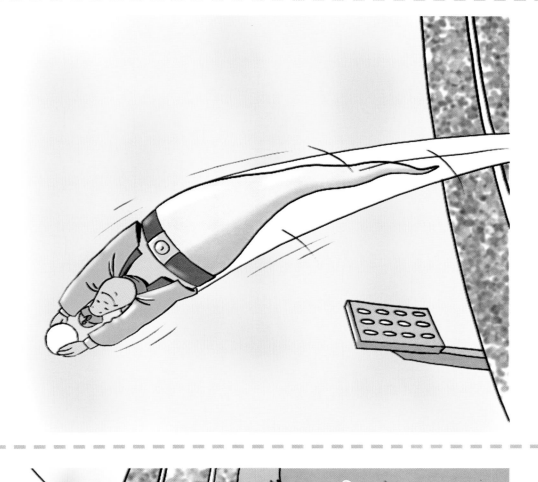

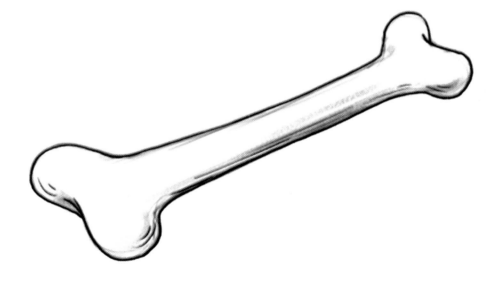

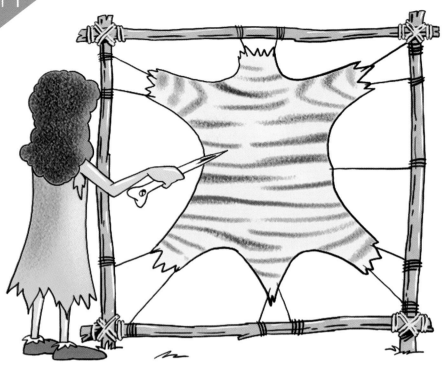

WEAPONS

CLOTHES

TOOLS

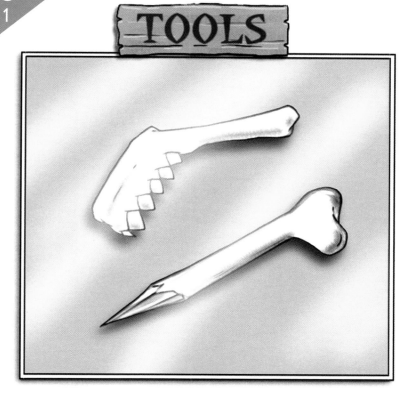

LAMPS

73

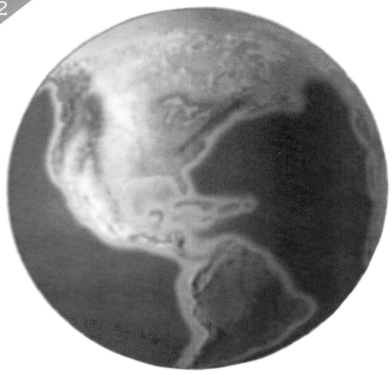

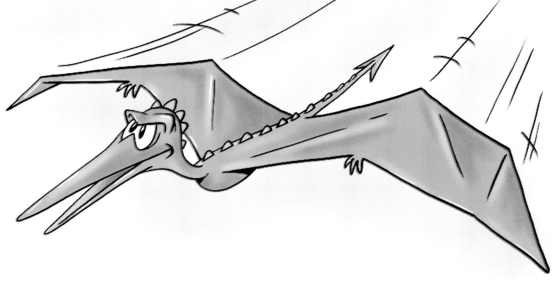

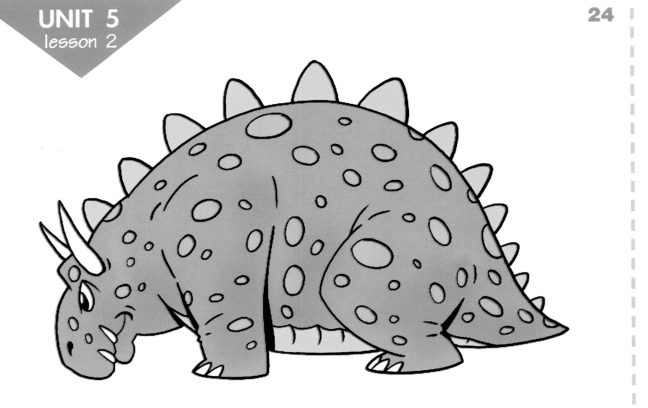

UNIT 6
lesson 1

UNIT 6
lesson 1

UNIT 6
lesson 1

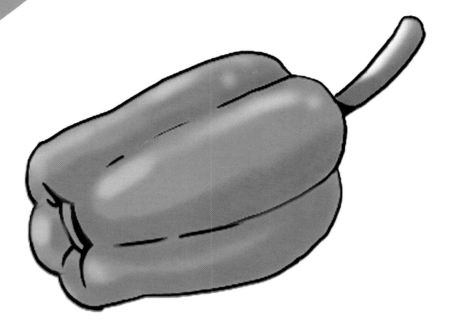

UNIT 6
lesson 1

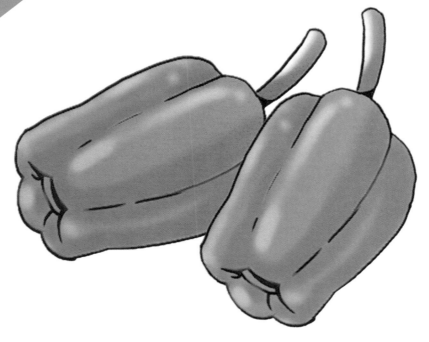

FLOUR

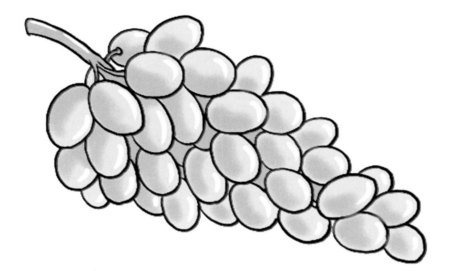

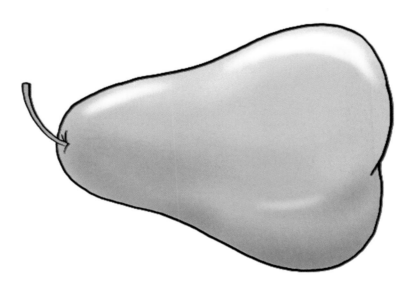

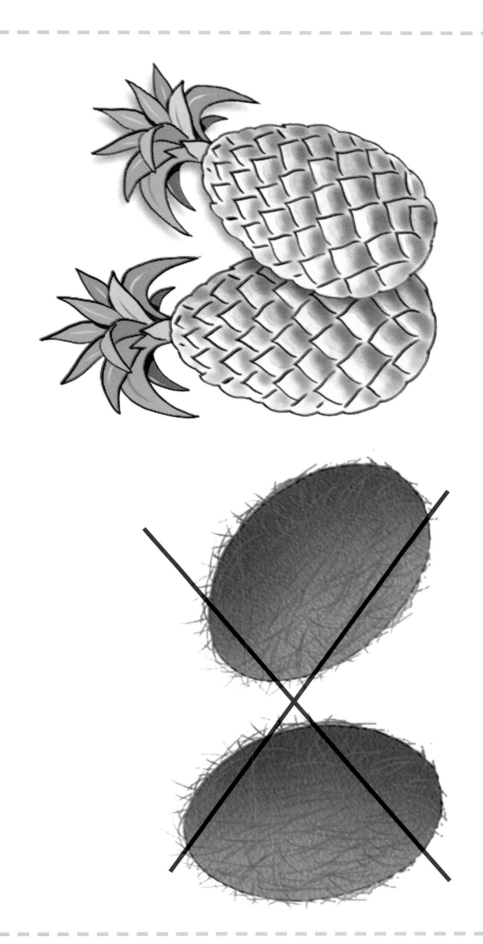

UNIT 6
lesson 2

UNIT 6
lesson 2

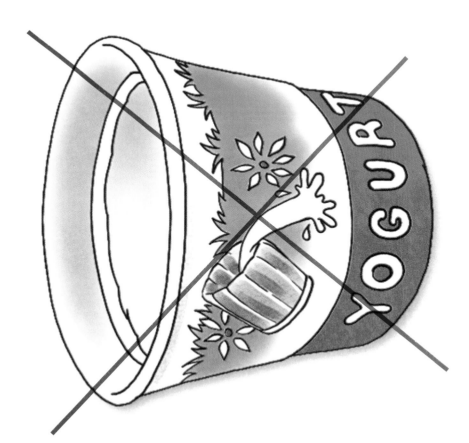

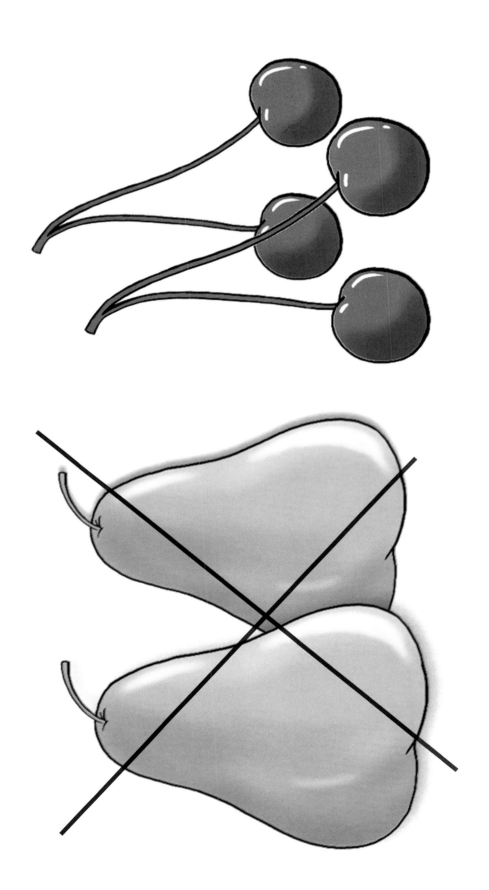

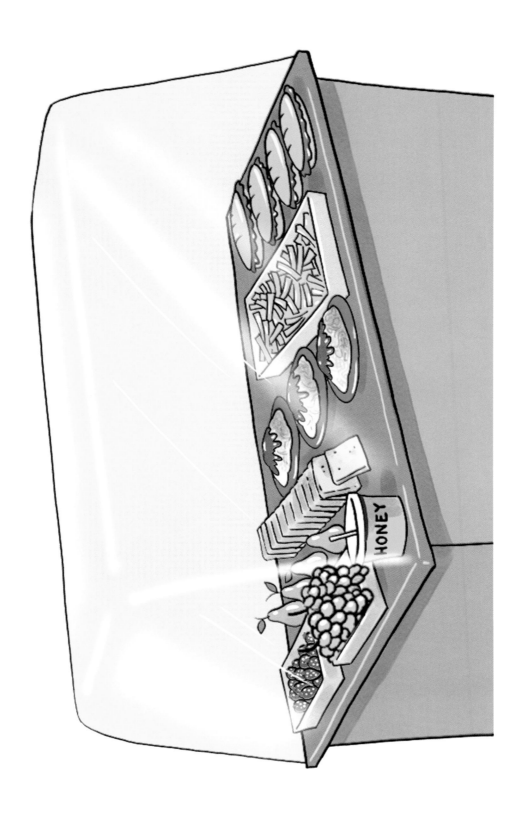

HONEY

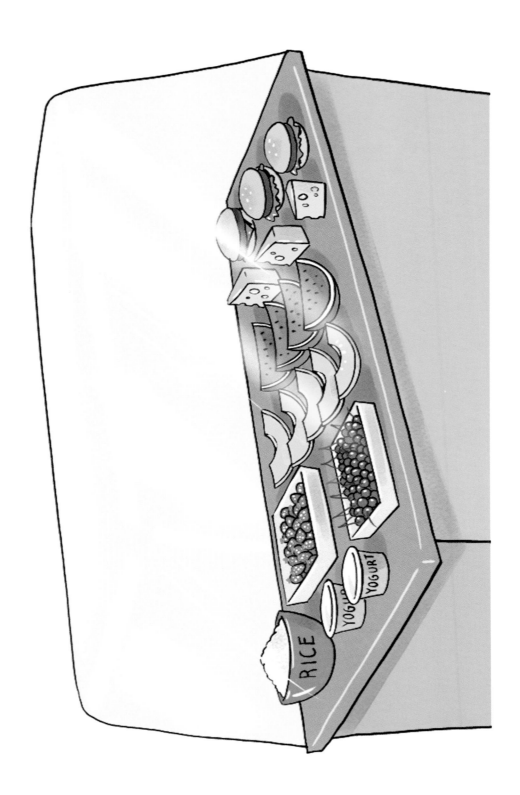

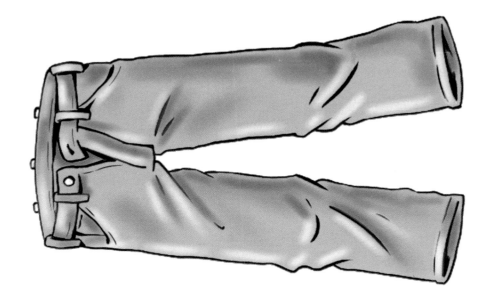

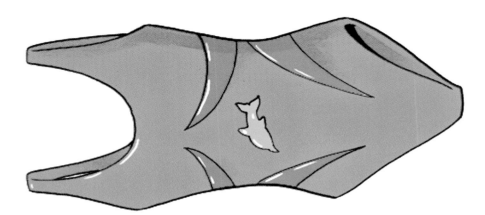

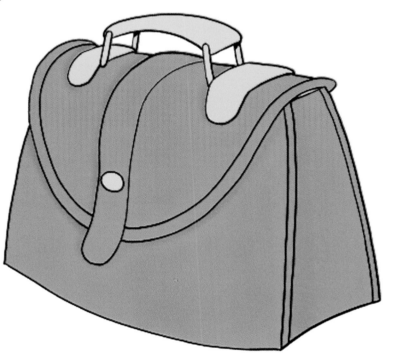

UNIT 7
lesson 1

UNIT 7
lesson 1

Chocolate

UNIT 7
lesson 2

UNIT 7
lesson 2

UNIT 7
lesson 2

25

UNIT 7
lesson 2

26

Rubrics for the Picture Flashcards

Unit 1 (flashcards 1 - 23)

Lesson 1   Ex. 1

1   field, grass

2   wool, sheep

3   cowboy

4   farm, bird, cow, snail, chicken, duck, goat

Lesson 1   Ex. 4

5   Cows are fatter than goats!

6   Horses are taller than sheep!

7   Snails are smaller than ducks!

8   Chickens are bigger than mice!

9   Cats are cleverer than birds!

Lesson 2   Ex. 1

10   forest, panda

11   grassland, cheetah

12   jungle, python

13   sea, whale

14   turtle

15   world, country

16   bamboo, leaf

17   slow

Lesson 2   Ex. 4

18   It's the oldest panda in the park!

19   It's the tallest giraffe in the park!

20   It's the biggest elephant in the park!

21   It's the oldest turtle in the park!

22 It's the fastest cheetah in the park!

23 It's the longest python in the park!

Unit 2 (flashcards 1 - 29)

Lesson 1   Ex. 1

1 sore throat

2 cough

3 headache

4 toothache

5 stomachache

6 cold

7 ill, socks, scarf

8 aspirin

9 put on

10 take off

11 pyjamas, slippers

Lesson 1   Ex. 4

12 I feel terrible! I've got a sore throat!

13 I feel terrible! I've got a headache!

14 I feel terrible! I've got a cough!

15 I feel terrible! I've got a stomachache!

16 I feel terrible! I've got a toothache!

17 I feel terrible! I've got a cold!

Lesson 2   Ex. 1

18 hurt

19 temperature

20 medicine

21 chest

22 jumper

23 ticket

24 sweets

25 You must be quiet!

26 You must turn on your light!

27 You must turn left!

28 You must buy a ticket!

29 You must turn off your radio!

Unit 3 (flashcards 1 - 29)

Lesson 1 Ex. 1

1 naughty

2 cute

3 noisy

4 quiet

5 dirty

6 show

7 circus

8 post office

9 library

Lesson 1 Ex. 4

10 Look at this photo! Wendy was very noisy!

11 Look at this photo! Cindy was very cute!

12 Look at this photo! Oscar was very quiet!

13 Look at this photo! Wendy was very naughty!

14 Look at this photo! Eddy was very funny!

15 Look at this photo! Lin was very clever!

16 Look at this photo! Tom was very dirty!

Lesson 1 Ex. 5

17 A: Was Jean at the library yesterday?
   B: No, she wasn't. She was at the post office.

18 A: Was George at the post office yesterday?

  B: No, he wasn't. He was at the restaurant.

19 A: Were Rick and Faye at the restaurant yesterday?

  B: No, they weren't. They were at the circus.

20 A: Were Carl and Sharon at the circus yesterday?

  B: No, they weren't. They were at the library.

<hr>

Lesson 1   Ex. 5

17 (Where was Jean yesterday?) Jean was at the post office.

18 (Where was George yesterday?) George was at the restaurant.

19 (Where were Rick and Faye yesterday?) Rick and Faye were at the circus.

20 (Where were Carl and Sharon yesterday?) Carl and Sharon were at the library.

<hr>

Lesson 2   Ex. 1

21 town, hospital, greengrocer's, butcher's, museum,police station, baker's

<hr>

Lesson 2   Ex.4

22 There was a greengrocer's.

23 There were a lot of small shops.

24 There was a museum.

25 There were a lot of small houses.

26 There was a post office.

27 There was a police station.

<hr>

Lesson 2   Ex. 6

28 There was a butcher's in Highton sixty years ago.

There was a post office in Highton sixty years ago.

There was a baker's in Highton sixty years ago.

There was a greengrocer's in Highton sixty years ago.

There was a school in Highton sixty years ago.

There was a library in Highton sixty years ago.

29 Oh, there isn't one now! But there's a supermarket.

Oh, there isn't one now! But there's a museum.

Oh, there isn't one now! But there's a cinema.

Oh, there isn't one now! But there's a hospital.

Oh, there isn't one now! But there's a bank.

Unit 4 (flashcards 1 - 30)

Lesson 1   Ex. 1

1 sports programme, boxing

2 comedy

3 cartoon

4 quiz show

5 the news

6 computer game

7 study

8 video

Lesson 1   Ex. 4

9 I watched a comedy on Channel 4.

10 I watched a cartoon on Channel 4.

11 I watched a sports programme on Channel 4.

12 I watched a quiz show on Channel 4.

13 I watched the news on Channel 4.

Lesson 2 Ex. 1

14 ring

15 seesaw, seal, bounce

16 kick

17 land

18 bucket

19 clap, laugh

Lesson 2 Ex. 4

20 Charlie walked into the ring with Sally.

21 Oscar played basketball with Eddy.

22 Wendy cycled in the park with Lin.

23 Jamal travelled to France with Masid.

24 Tom painted a picture with Bob.

Lesson 2 Ex. 5

25 (Where did Masid travel last week?)

Masid travelled to Planet Ziccom last week.

26 (Which team did Masid want to watch?)

Masid wanted to match his favourite soccer team.

27 (Who kicked the ball to Ziggy?)

Ziggor kicked the ball to Ziggy.

28 (Where did the ball land?)

The ball landed in Masid's popcorn.

29 (Where did Masid jump?)

Masid jumped in the air.

30 (Where did Masid land?)

Masid landed in the goal.

Unit 5 (flashcards 1 - 24)

Lesson 1   Ex. 1

1 cave, cavemen

2 strong, wood

3 stone

4 bone

5 dinosaur

6 hunt, weapon

7 animal skin, tool

8 Egypt, statue

Lesson 1   Ex. 4

9 They made weapons from wood!

10 They made clothes from animal skins!

11 They made tools from bones!

12 They made lamps from stones!

Lesson 2   Ex. 1

13 beak, wing

14 sun, cloud

15 dust

16 comet

17 hit

18 sharp claws, neck

19 earth

Lesson 2   Ex. 4

20 Look at its sharp teeth and claws!

21 Look at its long neck and tail!

22 Look at its short arms and legs!

23 Look at its big beak and wings!

24 Look at its big head and body!

Unit 6 (flashcards 1 - 25)

Lesson 1   Ex. 1

1 olive oil

2 cherry on top

3 green pepper

4 bake, oven

5 rich, poor

6 minute

Lesson 1   Ex. 4

7 A: How many tomatoes do you need?
  B: Not many!

8 A: How much cheese do you need?
  B: Not much!

9 A: How many onions do you need?
  B: Not many!

10 A: How much olive oil do you need?
   B: Not much!

11 A: How many green peppers do you need?
   B: Not many!

12 A: How much flour do you need?
   B: Not much!

Lesson 2 Ex. 1

13 grapes

14 pear

15 strawberry

16 honey, yogurt

17 salt and pepper

18 fry, saucepan, frying pan

Lesson 2   Ex. 4

19 I haven't got any grapes but I've got some strawberries.

20 I haven't got any coconuts but I've got some pineapples.

116

21 I haven't got any yogurt but I've got some honey.

22 I haven't got any pears but I've got some cherries.

23 I haven't got any pepper but I've got some salt.

Lesson 2   Ex. 6

24 T: Team A, is there any spaghetti in your picture?

Team A: Yes, there is some spaghetti in our picture.

T: Good. One point. Team B, is there any spaghetti in your picture?

Team B: No, there isn't any spaghetti in our picture.

T: No point, Team B.

25 T: Team A, is there any spaghetti in your picture?

Team A: Yes, there is some spaghetti in our picture.

T: Good. One point. Team B, is there any spaghetti in your picture?

Team B: No, there isn't any spaghetti in our picture.

T: No point, Team B.

Unit 7 (flashcards 1 - 26)

Lesson 1   Ex. 1

1   jeans

2   T-shirt

3   swimming trunks

4   swimsuit

5   sunglasses

6   trainers

7   suitcase

8   handbag

9   camp, camper

Lesson 1   Ex. 4

10   It's going to be hot!

11   It's going to be windy!

12   It's going to be rainy!

13   It's going to be cold!

14   It's going to be snowy!

15   It's going to be cloudy!

Lesson 2   Ex. 1

16   cabin

17   tent

18   motorbike

19   tired

20   supper

21   mat

Lesson 2   Ex. 4

22   We're going to go camping.

23   We're going to go sailing.

24   We're going to go swimming.

25   We're going to go fishing.

26   We're going to go skating.